It's My Money

A Kid's Guide to the Green Stuff

By Ann Banks

Illustrated by Susanna Natti

PUFFIN BOOKS

To my daughter, Kate Petre,
whose suggestions made this a better book.

PUFFIN BOOKS
Published by the Penguin Group
Penguin Books USA Inc., 375 Hudson Street, New York, New York 10014, U.S.A.
Penguin Books Ltd, 27 Wrights Lane, London W8 5TZ, England
Penguin Books Australia Ltd, Ringwood, Victoria, Australia
Penguin Books Canada Ltd, 10 Alcorn Avenue, Toronto, Ontario, Canada M4V 3B2
Penguin Books (N.Z.) Ltd, 182–190 Wairau Road, Auckland 10, New Zealand

Penguin Books Ltd, Registered Offices: Harmondsworth, Middlesex, England

First published in the United States of America by Puffin Books,
a division of Penguin Books USA Inc., 1993

1 3 5 7 9 10 8 6 4 2

Text copyright © Ann Banks, 1993
Illustrations copyright © Susanna Natti, 1993
All rights reserved

LIBRARY OF CONGRESS CATALOGING-IN-PUBLICATION DATA
Banks, Ann.
It's my money: a kid's guide to the green stuff / Ann Banks;
illustrated by Susanna Natti.   p.   cm.
ISBN 0-14-036086-7
1. Finance, Personal—Juvenile literature.   2. Money—Juvenile
literature.   I. Natti, Susanna, ill.   II. Title.
HG179.B295   1993   332.024—dc20   93-12618   CIP   AC
Printed in Mexico
Set in Cheltenham

About This Book

People talk about money a lot as you've probably figured out from listening to your parents' conversation. You might have heard them discussing money subjects that concern you directly, like the cost of piano lessons or Little League uniforms. And also subjects that have nothing to do with kids and that may bore you to death—like taxes or the price of gasoline. Money is an easy subject to get emotional about—and especially to argue about. In a family, everyone seems to have different ideas about how much should be spent, on what, and by whom.

One thing parents always tell kids is, "Money doesn't grow on trees." Say you express interest in the sneakers you saw on TV, the kind your best friend already owns—before long you're hearing that same old annoying money-doesn't-grow-on-trees lecture. And your parents probably heard the exact same thing from their parents. Parents can be counted on to think that kids have lots to learn about the value of a dollar. They have a point. Money will always play a part in your life, and knowing how to handle it takes practice—like riding a bicycle. The younger you start, the easier it will be.

Whether you have a little money or a lot, there are things you'll want to think about. How much spending money do you need each week? What's the best way to get a bigger allowance? Are there some big things you want to save for? In what ways would you like to earn money? Do you think you'd be good at selling, for example, or would you rather do extra chores? Are there ways you can use your money to help other people? *It's My Money* can help you figure out the answers to these and other questions. It isn't necessary to fill in every page; just look through the book and do the things that interest you. And if you'd rather do the projects in a different order, go right ahead. After all, it's your book.

Make Friends with Your Money

There are lots of funny nicknames for money: dough, bread, moola, bucks. Dollar bills are sometimes called greenbacks or smackers. Can you make up some more nicknames for money? Use your imagination and make them as silly as possible.

I think money should be called _____

_____

_____

Whose picture is on what money? To find the answers, ask your parents if you can examine the money in their wallets. Then draw lines to connect each bill with the person whose picture is on it.

1. One-dollar bill   a. Andrew Jackson

2. Five-dollar bill   b. George Washington

3. Ten-dollar bill   c. Abraham Lincoln

4. Twenty-dollar bill   d. Alexander Hamilton

4

Make Friends with Your Coins

Collect an example of each U.S. coin: a penny, a nickel, a dime, a quarter, a half-dollar—and, if you can find one, a Susan B. Anthony dollar coin. Do rubbings of the front and back of each coin on this page. (Put the coin underneath the page and rub lightly with a pencil until the image comes through.)

penny   nickel

dime   quarter

half-dollar   dollar

Money Dreams

Let's say you lucked into a lot of money and had to spend it on yourself and your friends. What would you do? Buy a horse? Take your friends to Disney World? Get some really cool clothes?

If I had $100 I'd spend it on _____

_____

_____

If I had $1,000 I'd spend it on _____

_____

_____

If I had $10,000 I'd spend it on _____

_____

_____

More Money Dreams

Compare your secret desires with someone else's. Ask the same questions of your mother or father, sister or brother, or your best friends.

If _____ had $100 he/she would spend it on _____

_____

If _____ had $1,000 he/she would spend it on _____

_____

If _____ had $10,000 he/she would spend it on _____

_____

If _____ had $100 she/he would spend it on _____

_____

If _____ had $1,000 she/he would spend it on _____

_____

If _____ had $10,000 she/he would spend it on _____

_____

Earning Money

So you want to earn some money of your own. Well, maybe you'd rather find it on the sidewalk, but you can't count on that. Basically, there are two ways to go about earning money: sell people something they want, or perform a service like dog walking or raking leaves.

If your parents are willing to hire you, you can try taking on extra chores at home. (These would be in addition to the regular chores that you already do.) Here are some possibilities. Why not offer to shine family members' shoes, for example? Or arrange the books on the bookshelf. Or help address party invitations. Or take over recycling chores.

My regular chores are:

_____

_____

_____

_____

_____

Extra jobs I can do around the house are:

_____

_____

_____

_____

_____

Jobs I Can Do

For doing _____ I will be paid _____

The rules of this job are _____

_____

_____

For doing _____ I will be paid _____

The rules of this job are _____

_____

_____

For doing _____ I will be paid _____

The rules of this job are _____

_____

_____

For doing _____ I will be paid _____

The rules of this job are _____

_____

_____

Rewards

Here's a way to earn money that's for kids only! Some parents are willing to pay rewards for behavior they want to encourage—practicing a musical instrument, for example, or reading a certain number of books. (If your parents aren't willing to pay cash rewards, don't fight it. There are plenty of other ways to earn money—read on for suggestions.)

If I keep my promise to _____

my parents agree to pay me _____

If I keep my promise to _____

my parents agree to pay me _____

If I keep my promise to _____

my parents agree to pay me _____

Earning Money Away from Home

There's a lot to be said for making money outside your home. It can give you a good feeling when someone who isn't a member of your family thinks you're responsible enough to hire for a job. But what job? Start by thinking of the kinds of jobs kids usually do in your neighborhood. Put an X by the jobs there is a demand for and a check by the jobs you think you'd like to do.

_____ Taking in mail

_____ Cat feeding

_____ Baby-sitting

_____ Running errands

_____ Dog walking

_____ Leaf raking

_____ Lawn watering

_____ Lawn mowing

_____ Weeding

_____ Snow shoveling

_____ Car washing

_____ Delivering newspapers

Other Jobs

If ordinary jobs don't appeal to you, or if there is no demand for them in your neighborhood, use your imagination. First, think about what you're good at and what you enjoy doing. Maybe you've been practicing a magic act, for example. All you need is a top hat and a cape and you're ready to start a business entertaining at kids' birthday parties. Or get together with your friends and put on a play—you can make money by charging admission and by selling refreshments. Are your butterscotch brownies famously delicious? Offer to cater the dessert at a neighbor's party. Do you love to draw or paint? Pick out some of your best work and have an art sale. Know some good jokes? Write them down on file cards and offer them for sale to friends and family.

I can use my talents to earn money by:

_____

_____

_____

_____

_____

My Business Plan

With some jobs, you have to spend before you can earn. Where will you get the money to pay expenses, and how can you know if you're making a profit? Figuring out the answers to these questions is part of making a business plan. Before you can bake something, for example, you will need to buy ingredients. If you already have a customer lined up, you might ask him or her to pay for the ingredients directly, plus an extra fee for your labor. Another method is to pay the expenses out of your own pocket, and then figure them in when you're deciding what to charge.

Either way, it's very important to keep a record of your work expenses: ingredients, equipment, advertising. Once you subtract your expenses from your total earnings, you'll know how much profit you have made.

My work expenses are: _____ $ _____

_____ $ _____

_____ $ _____

_____ $ _____

_____ $ _____

Total: $ _____ (A)

For my service or product I will charge: $ _____ (B)

My profit will be (B minus A): $ _____

How to Get Jobs

Once you've decided on the job you'd like to do, you need customers. First, tell everyone you can think of to spread the word—your piano teacher, your soccer coach, your pediatrician. And get your parents to tell their friends. Before you know it, someone will hire you.

Another way to get work is to show off your skills. Offer free samples of your brownies, for example. Make friends with your neighbors' cat—when they go away on vacation, you'll be the one to get the cat-sitting job. This works for neighbors' children, too. Even if you're not old enough to baby-sit, you can get a job entertaining little ones when their parents need to get something done at home. (And then by the time you are ready for solo baby-sitting, you'll have a ready-made employer.)

Do you have stuff you no longer want? If someone on your street is having a tag sale, ask for permission to join in. It's possible to make a surprising amount of money by selling off your used toys and games—and it's a form of recycling that benefits everyone. (Just be sure to check with your parents first; they may have their own ideas about what you should be getting rid of.)

If you like outdoor work—car washing, leaf raking, snow shoveling, lawn mowing—offer to do the job for your parents. When neighbors comment on how hard you're working, let them know you can be hired to do the same job for them.

Try advertising. Make a poster that explains what service you're offering and how you can be reached. (Be sure to check with your parents before giving out your phone number.) You can hang your poster on public bulletin boards in places like schools, doctors' offices, supermarkets, and libraries. When people call, it's a good idea to be ready with references, that is, names of people who know you and are willing to say that you are hardworking and reliable. You must ask these people ahead of time if it's okay to give out their names.

Use this page to design a job-wanted poster

LOOKING FOR A

_____ ?
(name of job)

_____ -year-old _____ needs work.
(your age)   (girl/boy)

I am experienced and reliable. Reasonable rates. References available.

Call _____ at _____ .
(your name)   (your phone number)

On the Job

Say you get a job feeding your neighbors' cats and watering their plants while they are away for a few days. You'll want to make sure that you and your employers agree on exactly what you're supposed to do, when you're supposed to do it, and how much you'll be paid. You can draw up an agreement that might say something like this:

I, _____ , agree to _____
_____(your name)_____   _____(description of job)_____

every_____ at _____ until _____.
   (how often)   *(what time)*   *(date the job is over)*

For this work I will be paid _____ per_____.
                               (amount)   *(day or week)*

In case of an emergency, I should call _____
                                               (name)

at _____ .
    (phone number)

Special instructions about how the job should be done are _____

_____

_____

_____

_____

_____

Allowance Time

Some kids get allowances. Some don't. In 1991 the magazine *Zillions: Consumer Reports for Kids* made a survey of over 700 kids around the country. About half the kids received a regular weekly allowance and half didn't. But *Zillions* also discovered that the kids who didn't get an allowance ended up with about the same amount of money every week—either from what their parents gave them or from odd jobs.

So which way is better? According to the survey, kids with allowances were happier with their money arrangements. They felt more grown-up when they didn't have to ask for money every time they needed something—or wanted something. Having an allowance also helped them learn to manage money and to save for something special.

So if you want an allowance, you have strong arguments you can make. But there's more to it than just convincing your parents to say yes. You also need to agree on the rules. Who will pay you and when? Is your allowance tied to doing chores? If so, what are they? What is your allowance supposed to pay for? (If you're expected to pay for things like movies or school supplies with your own money, for example, you'll need a big enough allowance to cover those expenses.)

Come up with good reasons for what you want, and you'll probably find that your parents are happy to negotiate with you. If everyone is satisfied, the plan has a better chance of working.

How Much?

This is *the* big question, and you'll want to be just as prepared as possible when the time comes to talk about it. (This is equally true if you're asking for an allowance raise.) One way to settle on what seems fair is to find out what other kids get. According to the *Zillions* survey, the typical allowance for 9- and 10-year-olds is $3 and for 11- and 12-year-olds, $5.

But that may not tell the whole story; for example, you may live in a part of the country where the cost of living is high. That could mean that you'd have to pay 50 cents for a candy bar that would cost a kid who lived someplace else only 35 cents. So it makes sense to do some surveying of your own by talking to friends and classmates. If they're willing to answer a few questions about their allowances, you can present these findings to your parents.

MY SURVEY

I talked to _____ kids about what they get for an allowance.
(how many)

What they told me is:

NAME	AMOUNT
_____	_____
_____	_____
_____	_____
_____	_____
_____	_____
_____	_____
_____	_____

Put a check mark next to the highest allowance and an X next to the lowest. You'll probably want to aim for an amount that is somewhere in between.

Do you mind answering questions on my allowance survey?

I don't get an allowance, but I do get treats.

Planning a Budget

In negotiating for your allowance, it also helps to have an idea of how much money you need. Write down what you expect to spend money on in a typical week and how much it will cost. Here are some of the things kids buy. Put a check mark next to the ones you want to include in your own budget.

____ Movie tickets

____ Candy and snacks

____ Magazines

____ Posters

____ Video games

____ Clothes

____ Paperbacks

____ Hobbies

____ Tapes

____ Sports equipment

Add your own items :

_____

_____

_____

_____

Besides the regular things you'll be spending your money on, there are extras like birthday and holiday presents for friends and family. Will you be expected to pay for those out of your allowance? If so, you'll need to include an amount for gifts in your budget. Talk to your parents about what they think is reasonable.

My Budget

Now make your own.

What to buy	Cost
_____	_____
_____	_____
_____	_____
_____	_____
_____	_____
_____	_____
_____	_____
_____	_____
_____	_____
_____	_____

Total amount of allowance needed: _____

Don't Forget Savings

Ask your parents if they're willing to add money for saving on top of your allowance. You'll need to agree about what the money is being saved for and when it can be spent. Maybe there is something specific that you want, like hockey skates or a new computer game. Or maybe you just want to save until you have a certain amount—and then decide what you want to do with the money.

The amount I'd like to save every week is _____

I plan to keep the money I save *(check one)*

☐ in my own savings account at the bank

☐ in a piggy bank at home

I'm saving up for _____ which costs about

_____ . Some of the ways I plan to get the money are _____

_____

_____

_____

_____

According to my calculations, it will take 3 months to save up for that doll bed. Wow!

Why don't you give me an allowance, too?

More Savings Goals

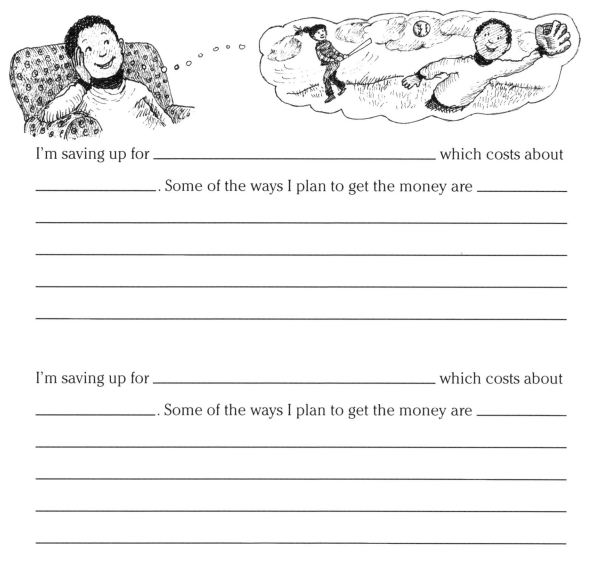

I'm saving up for _____ which costs about

_____. Some of the ways I plan to get the money are _____

_____

_____

_____

_____

I'm saving up for _____ which costs about

_____. Some of the ways I plan to get the money are _____

_____

_____

_____

_____

My Allowance Plan

When you and your parents have settled on an allowance plan, you might want to write it down here. That way, you'll have a record of what was agreed to.

_____
(today's date)

I, _____ , and _____ ,
    (your name)   *(your mother's or father's name)*

agree that _____ will receive a weekly allowance
              (your name)

of _____ . This allowance will be paid on _____
   (amount)   *(day of week)*

by _____ .
             (your mother's or father's name)

The amount of my allowance that I will save every week is _____ .

I agree not to spend the savings until _____ .

The amount and terms of my allowance will be renegotiated on _____ .
                                                           (date)

Signed by :

_____   _____
(your signature)   *(your parent's signature)*

Wish List

   You don't have to buy everything for yourself, of course. Thank goodness for birthdays, holidays, graduations, and other gift-giving occasions. If you keep a list handy of what you want, you'll never be stumped if someone asks. Show the list to your mother and father. Make your wishes as specific as possible; include sizes, colors, and brand names if these are important to you.

Things I would most like to get as presents are:

_____

_____

_____

_____

_____

_____

_____

_____

_____

The Old Days

Ask your parents, grandparents, aunts and uncles, and grown-up friends how things have changed since they were kids.

When _____ was my age, she/he got an allowance of ____

Some of the chores she/he did were _____

In those days a dollar would get you _____

Something she/he saved up to buy was _____

which cost _____

When _____ was my age, he/she got an allowance of ____

Some of the chores he/she did were _____

In those days a dollar would get you _____

Something he/she saved up to buy was _____

which cost _____

When _____ was my age, she/he got an allowance of ____

Some of the chores she/he did were _____

In those days a dollar would get you _____

Something she/he saved up to buy was _____

which cost _____

You didn't get an allowance?

I was expected to put money I got into the family jar.

25

When _____ was my age, he/she got an allowance of ____

Some of the chores he/she did were _____

In those days a dollar would get you _____

Something he/she saved up to buy was _____

which cost _____

When _____ was my age, she/he got an allowance of ____

Some of the chores he/she did were _____

In those days a dollar would get you _____

Something he/she saved up to buy was _____

which cost _____

When _____ was my age, he/she got an allowance of ____

Some of the chores he/she did were _____

In those days a dollar would get you _____

Something he/she saved up to buy was _____

which cost _____

I remember I wanted a china doll for my dollhouse....

Money Mistakes

Spending money is one of the easiest things in the world. Spending it wisely—in a way you'll be happy about a month later—is harder. Have you ever bought something because it looked good to you in the store or on the TV commercial? Then you get it home and find out it isn't as great as you thought, or you get sick of it in a big hurry. Or maybe you spend a lot of money on a shirt you really like. You're satisfied with what you bought, but then you see the same thing at another store selling for much less. Don't feel like a jerk. Nearly everyone has had experiences like these; it's called learning the hard way.

To prove it to yourself, ask your parents or your teachers or your neighbors or your grandparents.

_____ says the biggest money mistake she/he ever made was

_____ .

_____ says the biggest money mistake he/she ever made was

_____ .

_____ says the biggest money mistake she/he ever made was

_____ .

_____ says the biggest money mistake he/she ever made was

_____ .

Smart Spender

No one makes the right money choices all the time. But one method will help keep you happy with your decisions: never spend more than a dollar or two without thinking it over first. If a lot of money is involved, try waiting at least a week before buying. Sometimes you may find that in a day or so, you don't care about it that much anymore.

You can use the time to do some research about your intended purchase. Want a new computer game like the one your friend has? See if you can borrow his for an afternoon to see how much you really like it. If you know a kid who has something you think you'd like, ask if she'd recommend that you get it. What are the good things about it? What are the drawbacks?

Interested in some terrific-looking new sneakers you saw advertised on TV? Check them out in the store, and consider what else you could get for the money. If possible, look for the same item in several different stores and compare prices. Sometimes you can save a lot of money that way.

I think I might want to buy _____

The way I'm going to learn more about it is _____

_____

I think I might want to buy _____

The way I'm going to learn more about it is _____

_____

I think I might want to buy _____

The way I'm going to learn more about it is _____

_____

Get It for Less

If you decide you really want something, how much will you have to pay? That depends on where and when you buy it. Let's say you want a new pair of hockey skates. Christmas is coming, so you could put them on your wish list. Or you could buy them yourself in January when they probably will be on sale—costing maybe half as much as they did in December. Most big stores will mark things down to as little as half price a couple of times a year. If you want to find out when the next sale is scheduled, call the store and ask.

There are other possibilities as well. Kids outgrow skates, so you might try looking for a used pair at school sales, church sales, or yard sales. Other bargains at these sales: books and games.

If you want more clothes than your parents think you need, find out if your town has a kids' resale shop. Sometimes you can get a great-looking jeans jacket for not much more than the price of a movie ticket.

Ask your parents to help you figure out how to find the best bargains near you.

My bargain tips are _____

_____

_____

_____

_____

Fads and Other Good Ways to Spend Your Money

Your parents want you to learn to be responsible about your money, and not spend it foolishly. Of course you want that, too—but parents' ideas about what is foolish won't always be the same as your own. If most kids are wearing a certain thing, or collecting something, you'll want to check it out, too. If your parents call it a waste of money, listen to their point of view. Maybe they will convince you they're right. If they don't, well, it's your money. It's possible to get a lot of pleasure out of a fad. But just to remind yourself that what's hot one month is not the next, use this page to keep track of the latest fads.

Right now the big fad among my friends is _____

_____

The big fad before that was _____

_____

And before that _____

_____

Family Financial Decisions

All the money questions you face—what to buy, how much to save—are also questions your parents must answer when they're making the family budget. Ask them to share some of their questions with you; maybe they'd like to hear what you think.

The biggest budget question my parents have this year is _____

_____

_____

_____

_____

My opinion about this is _____

_____

_____

_____

_____

It would be nice to take that vacation, but we might have to replace the car.

Charity

One thing you can do with your money is to give some of it away to causes you believe in. You can donate to a fund to buy toys for homeless children, for example. You can contribute to the collection at your church or synagogue. You can give to an organization that is trying to stop pollution. Even if it is just a small amount of money, every little bit helps. And you'll have a feeling of satisfaction that you have done something to make a difference. Another way of giving is to donate your time as a volunteer. If this idea interests you, talk it over with your parents. Maybe they can help you get started.

These are the causes I would like to give money and/or time to this year:

_____

_____

_____

_____

_____

_____

_____

_____

There sure are a lot of causes that need help!

I'd like to make sure little kids have toys to play with.

I survived the Walk-a-thon

Rainforest

I'd like to make sure the air stays clean.

I'd like to make sure animals are taken care of.